D1261904

DRUGS AND THEIR DANGERS

E-CIGARETTES AND THEIR DANGERS

by Kari A. Cornell

BrightPoint Press

San Diego, CA

BrightP◇int Press

© 2020 BrightPoint Press
An imprint of ReferencePoint Press, Inc.
Printed in the United States

For more information, contact:
BrightPoint Press
PO Box 27779
San Diego, CA 92198
www.BrightPointPress.com

LIBRARY OF CONGRESS CATALOGING-IN-PUBLICATION DATA

Names: Cornell, Kari A., author.
Title: E-cigarettes and their dangers / by Kari Cornell.
Description: San Diego, CA : ReferencePoint Press, [2020] | Series: Drugs and their
    dangers | Audience: Grades 9 to 12. | Includes bibliographical references and
    index.
Identifiers: LCCN 2019003316 (print) | LCCN 2019005369 (ebook) | ISBN
    9781682827062 (ebook) | ISBN 9781682827055 (hardcover)
Subjects: LCSH: Electronic cigarettes--Juvenile literature. |
    Vaping--Juvenile literature. | Nicotine addiction--Juvenile literature. |
    Smoking--Health aspects--Juvenile literature.
Classification: LCC TS2260 (ebook) | LCC TS2260 .C675 2020 (print) | DDC
    362.29/6 |2 23
LC record available at https://lccn.loc.gov/2019003316

CONTENTS

FACT SHEET

- Between 2017 and 2018, the number of teens who used e-cigarettes increased by 75 percent.

- One Juul e-cigarette pod and twenty cigarettes contain the same amount of nicotine.

- Teens who vape are seven times more likely to start smoking.

- Vape pens were introduced in the United States in 2007 as a way for adults to quit smoking traditional cigarettes.

- Eighty percent of young people between the ages of 15 and 24 who try Juul keep using it.

- Popular companies include Blu, MarkTen XL, and Juul.

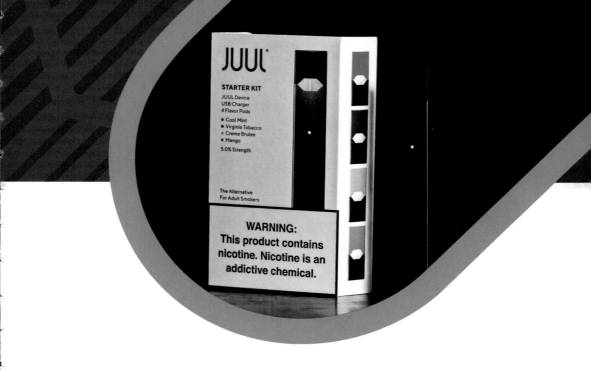

- In a 2016 study, 90 percent of those who tried to quit smoking by using e-cigarettes were still smoking after one year.

- Withdrawal symptoms from nicotine usually last three to four weeks.

- Sixty-six percent of teens don't know Juul pods contain nicotine.

MORE THAN FLAVORS

Julien Lavandier remembers the first hit he took off an e-cigarette. He was at a party. He was a sophomore in high school. It seemed like everyone was doing it. So he tried it too.

"At first it was a lot of, you know, chasing flavors, or doing smoke tricks," Lavandier explains. "And that was what really

E-cigarettes have become very popular among teens.

impressed me. I thought, you know, this is

cool, this looks like something fun."[1]

At school, kids vaped in the classroom.

Vaping is inhaling from an e-cigarette.

The teachers didn't know the vape pen wasn't a real pen. Lavandier guesses that about 25 percent of the kids at his high school vaped. He also took up smoking traditional cigarettes.

Juul is a brand of e-cigarette released in 2015. Juul flavor cartridges are small. They are packed with **nicotine**. A Juul looks like a USB flash drive. This makes it easy to hide. Juul has been wildly popular with teens. Lavandier got a Juul too. Then he found it "impossible to let go."[2]

That was more than three years ago. Now Lavandier is at college. He admits he

Vaping often leads teens to smoking cigarettes too.

takes as many as 300 puffs a day. He can't

go more than three days without vaping.

He's tried, but he hasn't been able to quit.

Lavandier isn't alone. The use of

e-cigarettes among high school students

jumped from 1.5 percent in 2011 to

Teens often don't know they are breathing nicotine into their lungs when they vape.

16 percent in 2015. Between 2017 and

2018, the number of teens who vaped

increased by 75 percent.

The US Food and Drug Administration (FDA) calls vaping an **epidemic**. Many teens do not know that a Juul is an e-cigarette. They don't understand that it contains nicotine. Of teens who use it, 66 percent think they are just vaping flavors such as bubble gum. The amount of nicotine in one Juul pod is equal to the amount found in twenty cigarettes. This jolt of nicotine makes e-cigarettes highly addictive. It doesn't stop with vaping. Teens who vape are seven times more likely to start smoking.

CHAPTER ONE

WHAT IS AN E-CIGARETTE?

E-cigarettes have many names. They are called vape pens, tanks, or pods. Sometimes they are called electronic nicotine delivery systems (ENDS). Vape pens were introduced in the United States in 2007. They were meant to help adults quit smoking cigarettes. They were thought to be safer than cigarettes. They would be

E-cigarettes come in many shapes and sizes.

used like nicotine patches. They provided

another way to get nicotine. The idea was

that users would smoke fewer cigarettes.

Since 2007, more than 460 brands of e-cigarettes have become available. The most popular is Juul. It is a newer brand. It hit stores in 2015. In 2018, the brand made up 72 percent of the e-cigarette market. Teens call vaping with a Juul pod "juuling."

HIDING IN PLAIN SIGHT

The device looks like a portable flash drive or a pen. It has a mouth piece at the top.

LOOKING COOL

The vaping device is designed to appeal to teens. Some combine with smartphones. Others look like small flashlights. Many vape pens can be personalized with patterned covers called skins.

Inside the device are heating coils. They warm the vape liquid. The liquid comes in a small cartridge. It slides into the device. Vape liquid comes in many different flavors. These liquids are called e-juice, e-liquid, or oil. They contain a mix of glycerin, nicotine, or marijuana. They also include flavoring chemicals.

The flavors are often fruity and candy-like. This appeals to kids. E-liquid is available in mango, mint, vanilla, bubble gum, and chocolate. There is even a flavor called "unicorn puke." These flavors mask the smell of other drugs in the e-liquid.

The smell can make it harder for adults to

detect these drugs.

E-cigarettes were invented in 2003 as a

substitute for traditional cigarettes. Chinese

pharmacist Hon Lik invented them. Burning

tobacco creates thousands of chemicals.

Manufacturers claimed e-cigarettes

SECRET INGREDIENTS

It's hard to know what's in an e-cigarette.
Before 2018, e-cigarette companies didn't have
to tell customers what was in their products.
Tests showed metals, flavoring additives, and
many chemicals in the oil. All of these may
become harmful when vaporized.

were safer. In the United States, e-cigarettes became a multibillion-dollar industry. Selling them became very profitable.

Some studies show smokers of traditional cigarettes try to use e-cigarettes to quit. Other studies show that many users vape for fun. This means users did not smoke before starting e-cigarettes. These users are not trying to quit. By vaping, they are becoming addicted to nicotine.

HOW VAPING WORKS

A user inhales from the mouthpiece of a device. The batteries power the heating coils. This warms the liquid in the cartridge.

E-cigarettes have several parts.

When the liquid gets hot enough, it turns into a vapor. The user then inhales the vapor. The vapor goes into their lungs.

Vaping liquid contains nicotine and other chemicals. Some of the chemicals are toxic. E-cigarettes have lower levels of some of these chemicals than traditional cigarettes. But the chemicals are still going in the body. They enter through the lungs. Tiny sacs called **alveoli** fill the lungs. Within seconds the vapor moves from the alveoli in the lungs into the bloodstream. The user begins to feel the effects of the drug almost immediately.

ADVERTISING AND PROFITS

E-cigarette manufacturers spend a lot of money on advertising. They spent $15.7 million in the first three months of 2013. And that money went a long way. As of 2014, almost 70 percent of teens had seen ads. Displays in stores were the most commonly seen ad. Over 35 percent of teens had seen ads on the internet.

Sales of products that contain nicotine have increased in recent years. But sales of traditional tobacco have stayed the same. E-cigarette sales have caused the increase. "The skyrocketing growth of young people's

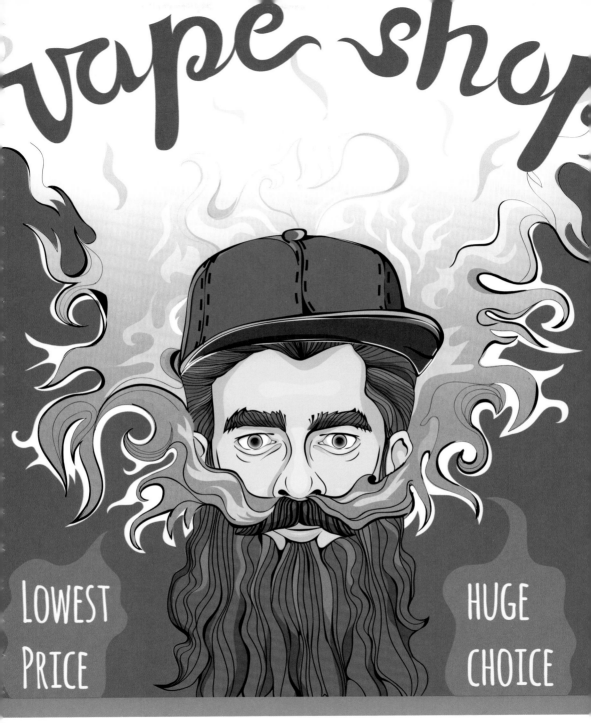

Vaping stores and companies spend a lot of money advertising their products.

Teen smoking has been on the decline for years, even before e-cigarettes became popular.

e-cigarette use over the past year threatens to erase progress made in reducing youth tobacco use," says Dr. Robert R. Redfield.[3] Redfield was the director of the Centers for Disease Control and Prevention (CDC).

CHAPTER TWO

WHAT IS NICOTINE'S EFFECT ON THE BODY?

Nicotine quickly enters the bloodstream. It makes the **adrenal glands** give off adrenaline. This is a hormone. Hormones are chemicals the body makes. They control bodily functions. Adrenaline makes the heart beat faster.

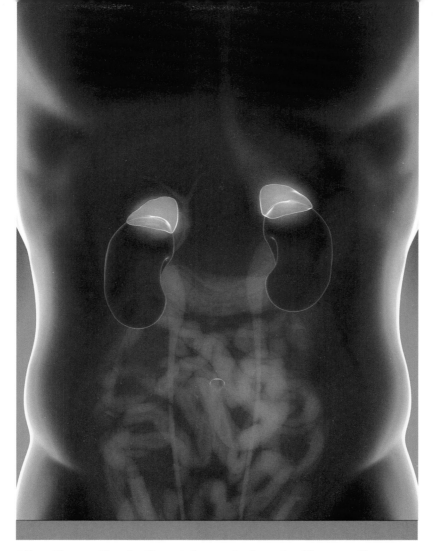

Nicotine affects the adrenal glands. These sit on top of the kidneys.

This speeds up breathing. It also increases

blood pressure. Blood pressure is how hard

the heart pumps blood.

Nicotine also triggers **receptors** in the brain. It causes them to make **dopamine**. Dopamine is a chemical that makes the body feel good. The adrenaline and dopamine make users feel alert and happy. The good feelings make the person want more nicotine. When a person takes nicotine, receptors react more strongly to the drug. These receptors release more dopamine. The person needs more nicotine to feel good.

NICOTINE AND THE DEVELOPING BRAIN

Nicotine is more harmful to teens than adults. This is because the teenage brain

Nicotine can have bad effects on teens' brains.
This can affect schoolwork.

is still developing. In fact, it doesn't stop developing until age twenty-five.

Nicotine use can lead to changes in parts of the brain. One of the affected areas controls attention span. Changes here can cause mood and attention problems. This means teens who vape may become depressed. They may also have trouble focusing in school. Nicotine use can affect the way the brain remembers too. These effects can harm users' schoolwork.

Vaping nicotine also affects the way the brain controls impulses. An impulse is the urge to do something. Having less control over impulses can be dangerous. Teens

may make risky decisions.

VAPING MAY LEAD TO OTHER DRUGS

The nicotine in many e-cigarettes can

make users seek more nicotine elsewhere.

Another place to get it is in regular

cigarettes. Teens are more likely to try

cigarettes if they vape.

VAPING ON THE RISE

The use of traditional cigarettes is at an all-time low among teens. The percentage of teens who smoked cigarettes dropped from 28 percent in 1998 to 8 percent in 2014. But vaping is on the rise. About 20 percent of students vaped in 2018.

Regular nicotine use can put users at risk for trying other drugs. Researchers have found that nicotine use actually changes the body's DNA. These changes make the effect of stronger drugs more appealing. Such drugs include cocaine and meth. These two drugs have similar effects to nicotine. They make the user feel good. He or she may feel more alert. However, these drugs are much more dangerous.

WHAT IS IN VAPE OIL?

For many years users didn't know what was in their vape oil. It contains fewer chemicals than traditional cigarettes. The oil contains

Vape oils have toxic chemicals. When the oils are heated, new chemicals also form.

lower levels of the chemicals it does

contain. People think it is less harmful. But

having fewer chemicals doesn't mean it is

harmless. Toxic chemicals are still present.

Vape oils contain formaldehyde and acrolein. Formaldehyde is a carcinogen. This means it causes cancer. Acrolein is used to kill weeds. Breathing it in damages the lungs.

When vape oils are heated, they give off nickel and chromium. Both of these chemicals are toxic. They can cause lung disease. The oils may also include cadmium. Cadmium is a toxic metal. It is blamed for breathing problems. Cadmium poisoning can lead to cancer and kidney failure. Cadmium can also damage users' bones.

POPCORN LUNG

Flavored oils contain other harmful chemicals. Diacetyl is used to create flavors in e-cigarettes. It is also used to give microwave popcorn its buttery taste. Workers at microwave popcorn factories have gotten sick from breathing it in. The sickness is called popcorn lung. The American Lung Association says popcorn lung is "a scarring of the tiny air sacs in the lungs resulting in the thickening and narrowing of the airways." Teens who use oils with diacetyl can get popcorn lung.

"Popcorn Lung: A Dangerous Risk of Flavored E-Cigarettes," American Lung Association, *July 7, 2016. www.lung.com.*

To create vapor, vape oils contain aerosols. These chemicals enter the lungs when a person vapes. Aerosols irritate the lungs, throat, and eyes. Aerosols also

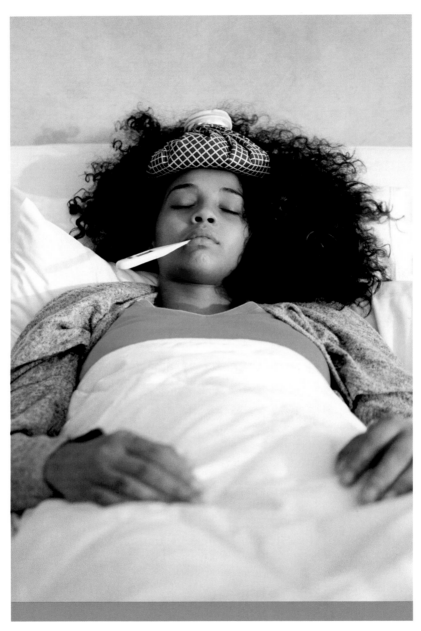

Teens who vape can get sick more easily than teens who don't.

weaken the body's ability to fight illness.

People who vape are more likely to catch a

cold or the flu.

ADDICTION

Teens who vape are exposed to many

harmful chemicals. And many of these

chemicals can make them sick if they

vape regularly. But one of the most serious

dangers of vaping is **addiction**. Nicotine

is very addictive. Teens who start vaping

usually don't stop. In fact, 80 percent

of young people between fifteen and

twenty-four who try a Juul keep using it.

This increases the chances of addiction.

Addiction also causes lasting effects on brain development. It can make it harder to concentrate and learn. This can affect teens' time at school. Doing poorly in school can have lifelong consequences too.

Addiction can make school harder for teens.

CHAPTER THREE

HOW DOES VAPING AFFECT PEOPLE AND SOCIETY?

N icotine is addictive. And most vaping devices contain at least some nicotine. Even vape oils that claim to be nicotine free have some nicotine. There is a lot of nicotine in Juul cartridges. This puts teens at high risk for addiction. In 2018

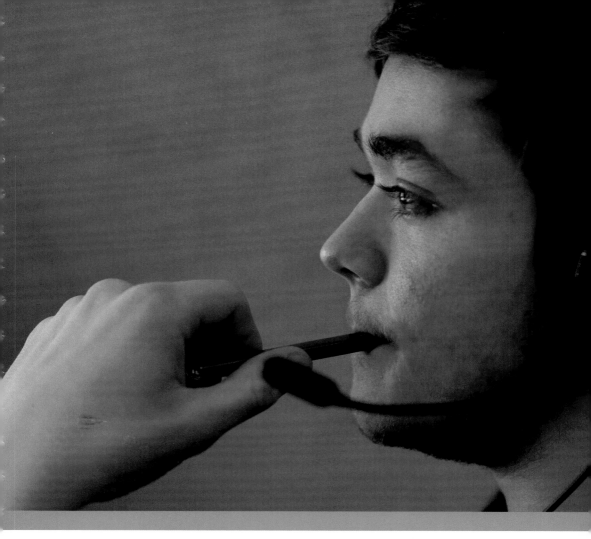

If teens are addicted, they will vape even while doing other activities, such as playing video games.

alone, 37.3 percent of high school seniors

said they vaped in the past year. This is a

big increase from 2014. About 13.4 percent

of teens vaped in 2014. Parents and doctors are alarmed. It is a dangerous trend.

Scott Gottlieb was the head of the FDA in 2018. This government agency tests the safety of drugs and medical products. This includes medicine, food, and other areas of public health. Gottlieb said, "The FDA won't tolerate a whole generation of young people

CAN E-CIGARETTES HELP ADULTS QUIT SMOKING?

E-cigarettes were meant to help adults quit regular cigarettes. But there is no proof that e-cigarettes help adults stop smoking. In a 2016 study, 90 percent of those who tried to quit with e-cigarettes were still smoking after one year.

becoming addicted to nicotine."[4] But this could be what is happening.

WHAT IS ADDICTION?

Addiction happens when the body needs the drug in the system to work properly. Nicotine changes what happens in the brain's reward center. Normally, when the body feels pleasure, the reward center releases dopamine. But when nicotine enters the bloodstream, it triggers a flood of dopamine. The dopamine makes the user feel happy and excited. The brain learns that vaping leads to more dopamine. The brain

Once smokers are addicted, they need to keep smoking just to feel normal.

connects vaping to feeling good. Now the brain pushes the user to get more nicotine.

Over time the brain gets used to the dopamine levels. Nerve cells in the brain adjust by making less dopamine. Now there is less dopamine in the brain's reward system. Users need to smoke to keep normal levels. The person no longer feels happy. They may not feel much of anything at all. They may not enjoy doing anything. Even activities that were once fun may be boring. If they take a higher dose of nicotine, though, they feel great again. This is called **tolerance**. But if users don't take nicotine, they feel awful. Their brain

needs the nicotine to feel normal. This

is addiction.

HOW DO YOU KNOW IF YOU ARE ADDICTED TO NICOTINE?

One sign of addiction is craving the drug.

To crave means to want more. People

who vape might be addicted to nicotine

if they cannot go more than two hours

without vaping.

Another sign is not being able to stop. It

is hard to control a craving. A person may

begin vaping several times each day. Vaping

may start to get in the way of friendships,

If users cannot get through normal activities without smoking, they are addicted to nicotine.

family, school, or work. Still, the user

continues doing it.

Someone who is addicted to nicotine

begins to feel bad when he or she

doesn't vape. This is called **withdrawal**.

Withdrawal happens when the body does

not have enough of the drug. Withdrawal

symptoms begin to appear within a few

hours. The person may have a headache.

He or she may feel anxious, irritable,

restless, and distracted. A user experiencing

HOW LONG DOES WITHDRAWAL LAST?

Withdrawal symptoms are the worst at two days after the last use. They can make a person feel miserable. These symptoms usually last three to four weeks. When the person stops using nicotine, the body slowly adjusts. The amount of dopamine it produces eventually returns to normal levels.

withdrawal can become depressed, frustrated, angry, and hungry. Many times, a user who is trying to quit nicotine can't sleep. He or she wants to vape to feel good again.

HOW DOES VAPING AFFECT SOCIETY?

Vaping is still a new way of taking nicotine. More study needs to be done. Researchers don't yet know how it will affect society. But they can get some idea from studying the effects of cigarettes.

Cigarette smoking has been linked to many diseases. They include cancer, heart disease, and lung disease. Smoking causes

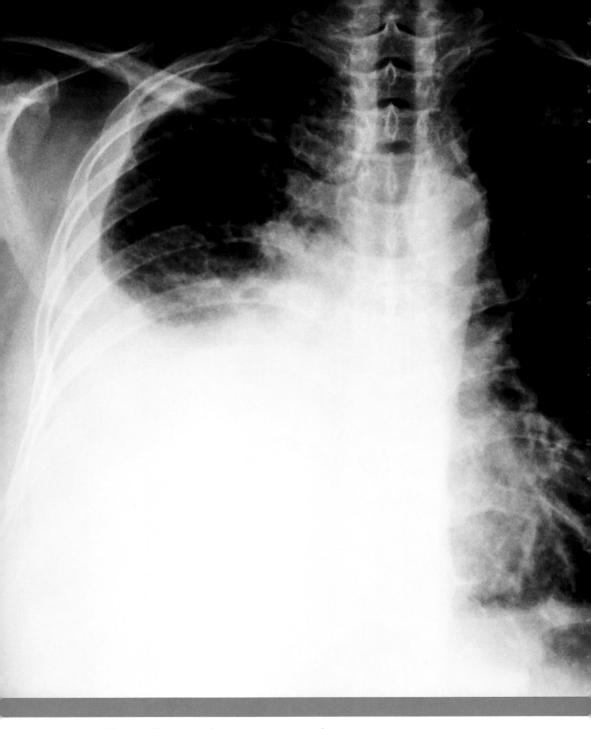

Cigarette smoke can cause lung cancer.
This shows up in X-rays of the lungs.

more preventable diseases and death than anything else. Nearly 500,000 Americans die from smoking-related diseases every year. The cost of smoking adds up. It affects everyone. Sick days from illnesses caused by smoking costs $150 billion in lost productivity annually. This means that less work is completed. Workers might not get paid for sick days. Smoking also costs Americans $130 billion in health care expenses each year.

Cigarettes have different effects than e-cigarettes. E-cigarettes lack tobacco. But they share many things too. Both use nicotine to addict users. And using e-cigarettes often leads to smoking cigarettes.

SECONDHAND SMOKE AND VAPOR

Even people who don't vape are affected. They are affected by those who vape around them. Secondhand smoke from vaping is toxic. The vapor has fewer chemicals than traditional cigarettes. Because of this, it may be less harmful than cigarette smoke. But users and people nearby are still breathing in harmful chemicals. These include formaldehyde and metal particles.

The same toxins that users breathe go into the air where others breathe them too.

Secondhand smoke from cigarettes

can cause more harm than smoking itself.

Smokers inhale through a filter. The filter

absorbs some of the harmful chemicals.

But secondhand smoke doesn't go through

a filter. Exposure to secondhand smoke has been linked to cancer. It also increases the chances of a heart attack or stroke. Secondhand vape smoke has many of the same risks. A European study found increased levels of several chemicals in the air. It looked at what chemicals were in the air after e-cigarette use. The study found aluminum, nicotine, and other dangerous chemicals. These chemicals have been linked to cancer and heart disease.

Children who are exposed to secondhand smoke are more likely to get sick. They are at higher risk for getting

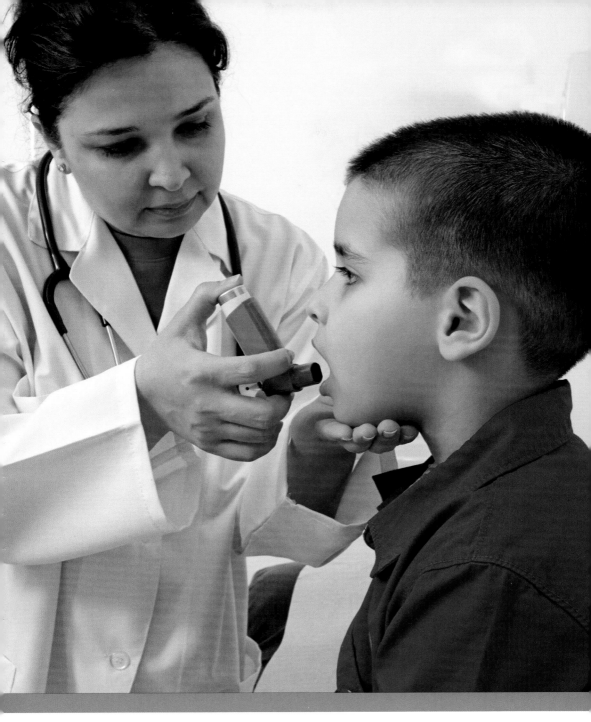

Secondhand smoke can cause breathing problems in children.

Going to the doctor adds to the cost of using e-cigarettes.

pneumonia and bronchitis. They experience

more asthma attacks. They also get

more ear infections. Babies who live with

smokers are at higher risk for sudden infant

death syndrome. This is when infants die in

their cribs without a visible reason.

The costs of illnesses add up as well.

Trips to the doctor can get expensive.

Parents might have to take time off work to

care for sick children. These are all good

reasons to quit vaping.

CHAPTER FOUR

WHAT ARE TREATMENTS FOR E-CIGARETTE ADDICTION?

Vaping is relatively new. But nicotine addiction is not. Many of the same treatments work for both cigarettes and vaping. Medication is sometimes used for adults. However, this has not been proven to help teens. More research is needed.

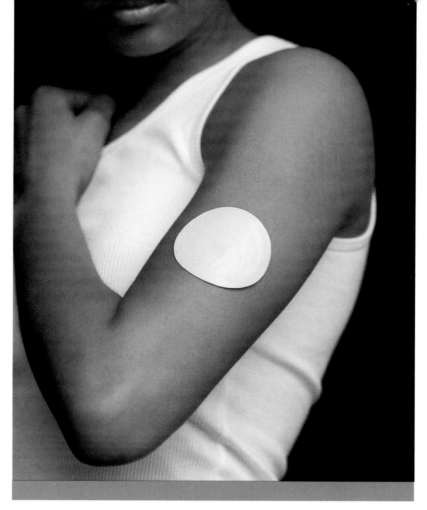

Nicotine addiction is hard to break. Many people use nicotine patches or gum to help them quit.

THERAPY

Seeing a trained therapist is one way to

quit. It is one of the most effective methods.

Therapists help to change behaviors that

make teens want to vape. This type of

therapy is called behavioral treatment. It

teaches teens how to cope with cravings.

Instead of vaping, they learn positive things

to do instead. There are three different

types of behavioral treatments. One is

cognitive-behavioral therapy (CBT). The

second is motivational interviewing (MI). The

third is mindfulness. The treatments can

work well together.

CBT teaches skills to cope with cravings.

This helps the person learn positive

behaviors. They create better habits.

Different forms of therapy can be very helpful for people overcoming addiction.

This helps them resist cravings and quit using nicotine.

MI begins with talking about how quitting makes the user feel. The therapist focuses on why the person decided to quit. Together, the therapist and patient set goals. They make plans to achieve them. They talk through pros and cons of using nicotine. They also talk about change.

Mindfulness has become more popular in recent years. This approach teaches the person to focus on what makes him or her want to vape. The person faces these urges head on. Then he or she can work through them. The person learns ways to

tolerate cravings.

WHAT IS THE GREATER COMMUNITY DOING TO STOP VAPING?

People are trying to keep e-cigarettes away

from teens. Vaping laws vary between

states. As of March 2019, people under age

PERSONALIZED SUPPORT

Support during cravings is key to quitting nicotine. There are different kinds of support. The best choice depends on the person. It may be advice from a counselor. It could be a call to a helpline. For teens, text messaging may be effective. Social media can help too.

eighteen cannot buy e-cigarettes in most states. Other states have a minimum age of nineteen or twenty-one. In many states, it is against the law for teens to have an e-cigarette. Many schools have banned e-cigarettes.

In August 2016, the FDA announced a new policy. It would begin to restrict e-cigarettes. This affected all e-cigarettes sold since February 2007. All e-cigarettes needed FDA approval. While waiting for review, the products could still be sold.

Under the new rules, stores can't sell vaping supplies to minors. They also can't

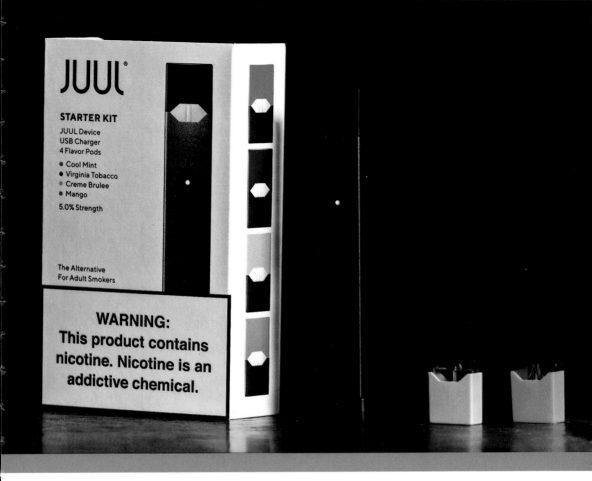

Some flavors appeal to kids. The FDA has made companies take steps to keep these flavors away from teens.

hand out samples. Vaping companies

must include warning labels. They must list

ingredients on packages. And they cannot

claim health benefits without proof.

To curb teens' use, the FDA also released ads. They were targeted toward teens. The ads appeared in schools. They showed up on social media. The ads were not played on television. The FDA did not want to scare away adults. Adult users may want to use vaping to quit smoking.

THE PUBLIC DEMANDS MORE

Some health groups called for more action. On April 18, 2018, they urged the FDA to step in. They wanted to fight underage use. The groups made requests. They asked that the FDA stop internet sales of Juul. They wanted stores to stop selling

With the increase in vaping, even the CDC has taken a stance on the subject.

to minors. They asked that the FDA make new rules about e-cigarettes by 2022. The FDA would decide if existing e-cigs could remain available.

US senators also made requests. They asked that the FDA make new rules.

These rules would stop companies from making flavors aimed at kids. There is a similar ban on flavored cigarettes.

The FDA responded within a week. It worked harder to stop underage sales. It sent people undercover into stores to buy e-cigarettes. It also restricted online sales. Finally, the FDA asked Juul to make plans to prevent teen use.

The FDA continued its efforts in 2018. In September, the FDA made an announcement. It said major vaping brands needed plans to prevent teens from vaping. They had sixty days to make these plans.

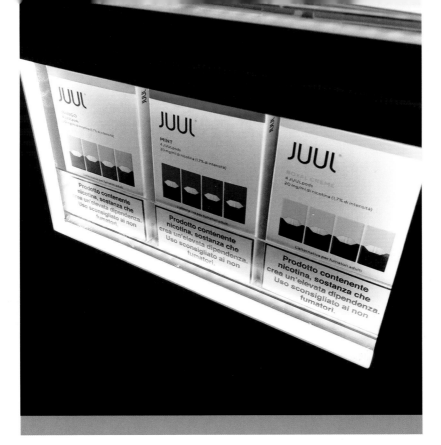

The FDA has targeted some e-cigarette flavors. Traditional cigarette flavors, such as menthol, have not been targeted.

The brands included Juul, Vuse, Blu, and Logic. If they didn't make those plans, the FDA would ban sales of some vaping flavors. Those that appeal to children would be banned.

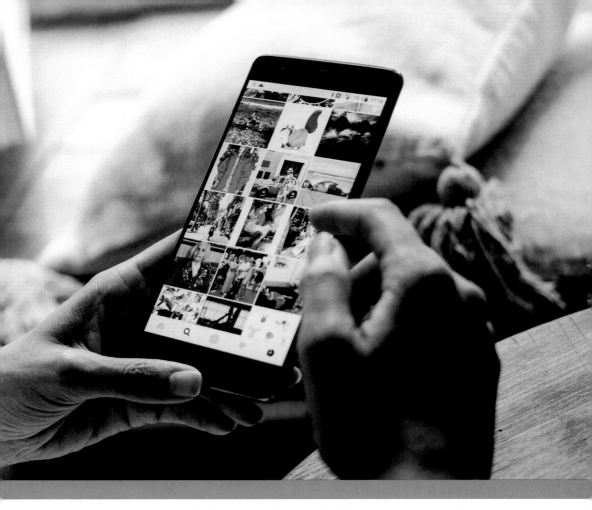

*Because social media is central in many teens'
lives, Juul deleted its social media accounts.*

Juul pulled most flavors from

convenience stores. These stores could

sell only tobacco, mint, and menthol. All

flavors are still available in specialty stores.

These stores sell smoking products. Juul also added more online age checks. It deleted its social media accounts. Juul's CEO is Kevin Burns. He said, "Our intent was never to have youth use Juul products. But intent is not enough. . . . the numbers tell us underage use of e-cigarette products is a problem. We must solve it."[5]

In November 2018, the FDA planned a new ban. It would block the sale of sweet-flavored smoking products in convenience stores. Menthol and mint would still be available. The FDA would also have stricter age rules for online sales.

Scott Gottlieb of the FDA said, "We'll continue to base our actions on the best available science. And when it comes to protecting our youth, we'll continue to actively pursue a wide range of . . . actions. We'll leave no stone unturned."[6]

WHAT'S TO COME

The FDA has taken steps to prevent teens from vaping. Still, researchers need more information. Vaping's full effects are still not known. Vaping companies now have to list ingredients. The ingredients in some oils are dangerous. And new chemicals are created during vaping. Flavors can react with chemicals. These reactions could be dangerous. They would not be listed in the ingredients. But what is known has doctors concerned. Dr. Suchitra Krishnan-Sarin works at Yale Medicine. She says, "Parents should base their information on accurate

SAN FRANCISCO STEPS UP

In June 2018, San Francisco, California, took action. It became the first US city to ban the sale of flavored tobacco products. The ban includes vaping liquid. It also includes some cigarettes and cigars. About 68 percent voted in favor of the ban. It was called Proposition E. Since then nearby cities have passed similar bans.

facts and also encourage their children to read about and understand the science on this issue instead of relying on what their friends and peers tell them."[7]

The nicotine in e-cigarettes is addictive. It is also costly and harmful. It can hurt brain development. E-cigarettes can may help people quit using regular cigarettes. But it is best for teens never to try e-cigarettes.

Parents should talk to their teens about the dangers of e-cigarettes.

GLOSSARY

addiction

dependence on a substance, thing, or activity

adrenal glands

organs that produce hormones like adrenaline

alveoli

tiny air sacs in the lungs that allow people to breathe

dopamine

a chemical released by nerve cells in the body that sends signals to other nerve cells and makes the body feel good

epidemic

an outbreak of disease in a community at a particular time

nicotine

an addictive chemical found in the tobacco plant

receptor

a cell that responds to chemicals or hormones in the body

tolerance

ability to endure a substance

withdrawal

the process of stopping taking a drug

SOURCE NOTES

INTRODUCTION: MORE THAN FLAVORS

1. Quoted in John Daley, "He Started Vaping as a Teen and Now Says the Habit Is 'Impossible to Let Go,'" *NPR*, June 7, 2018. www.npr.org.

2. Quoted in Daley, "He Started Vaping as a Teen and Now Says the Habit Is 'Impossible to Let Go.'"

CHAPTER ONE: WHAT IS AN E-CIGARETTE?

3. Quoted in Kevin Lora, "Use of E-cigarettes Among Teens Is 'Exploding,'" *Consumer Reports*, February 13, 2019. www.consumerreports.org.

CHAPTER THREE: HOW DOES VAPING AFFECT PEOPLE AND SOCIETY?

4. Quoted in "FDA Calls Teen Vaping an 'Epidemic,' Threatens to Pull Products Off the Market," *CBS News*, September 12, 2018. www.cbsnews.com.

CHAPTER FOUR: WHAT ARE TREATMENTS FOR E-CIGARETTE ADDICTION?

5. Quoted Ryan W. Miller, "Juul to Halt Sale of Flavored E-Cigarette Products in Stores After FDA Crackdown," *USA Today*, November 13, 2018. www.usatoday.com.

6. Scott Gottlieb, "Statement from FDA Commissioner Scott Gottlieb, M.D., on Proposed New Steps to Protect Youth by Preventing Access to Flavored Tobacco Products and Banning Menthol in Cigarettes," *FDA*, November 15, 2018. www.fda.gov.

7. Quoted in Kathleen Raven, "Your Teen Is Underestimating the Health Risks of Vaping," *Yale Medicine*, December 19, 2018. www.yalemedicine.org.

FOR FURTHER RESEARCH

BOOKS

Carol Hand, *Tobacco*. Minneapolis, MN: Abdo Publishing, 2019.

Peggy J. Parks, *The Dangers of E-Cigarettes*. San Diego, CA: ReferencePoint Press, 2017.

Christine Wilcox, *E-Cigarettes and Vaping*. San Diego, CA: ReferencePoint Press, 2016.

INTERNET SOURCES

Leigh Hopper, "New E-cig Study Shows Vaping Is No Deterrent to Teen Smoking," *USC News*, November 5, 2018. https://news.usc.edu.

"Quick Facts on the Risks of E-cigarettes for Kids, Teens, and Young Adults," *Centers for Disease Control and Prevention*, March 11, 2019. www.cdc.gov.

"Teens and E-Cigarettes," *National Institute on Drug Abuse*, February 2016. www.drugabuse.gov.

WEBSITES

Center for Disease Control and Prevention
https://e-cigarettes.surgeongeneral.gov

This site gives statistics and information about the dangers of teens using e-cigarettes.

National Institute on Drug Abuse: Tobacco, Nicotine, & E-Cigarettes
https://teens.drugabuse.gov

This site includes information about drugs such as nicotine and e-cigarettes and how they affect the body, as well as video games and blog posts geared toward teen readers.

smokefreeteen
https://teen.smokefree.gov

This site has information for teens about smoking and how to quit smoking.

INDEX

IMAGE CREDITS

ABOUT THE AUTHOR

Kari A. Cornell is a writer and editor who likes to cook, craft, and tinker in the garden. She has written many books for kids and teens, including *The Nitty Gritty Gardening Book*, *Dig In: 12 Easy Gardening Projects Using Kitchen Scrap*s, and *The Craft-a-Day Book*.